Musical Fingers

BOOK 1
BOOK 2
BOOK 3 ●
BOOK 4

by Frances Clark, Louise Goss and Sam Holland

ISBN 0-913277-11-8

Summy-Birchard Inc.
exclusively distributed by
Alfred Publishing Co., Inc.
16320 Roscoe Blvd., Suite 100
P.O. Box 10003
Van Nuys, CA 91410-0003

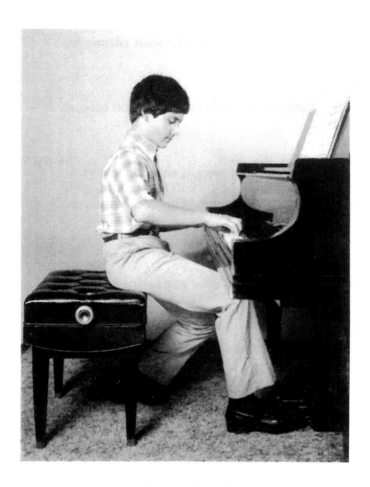

To the Student

Musical Fingers 3 is the third in a series of four books designed to help you develop the physical skills to play the piano. We call these books *musical* fingers because each exercise has musical as well as technical goals.

As you learned in Books 1 and 2, technic is a study of the way to produce the sounds you want to make at the piano. It includes developing skills in three areas:

-the ability to create in your imagination the *sound* you want to make;

-an awareness of the way your hands and body *look* to make that sound;

-an awareness of how your hands and body *feel* to make that sound.

Readiness to Play

To be ready to play, your body must be in an active and balanced state, free to move quickly and gracefully to any position on the keyboard. To insure physical readiness, there are several important checkpoints:

1. Height of the bench

Be sure the bench is the proper height for you, so that your upper arms hang loosely from your shoulders, and your forearms and wrists are level with the floor.

2. Distance from the keyboard

Be sure the bench is the proper distance from the keyboard, so that your elbows are free and at a comfortable distance from your body.

3. Posture

Sit tall, with your back straight, leaning very slightly toward the keyboard, and be sure that your shoulders are dropped and relaxed.

4. Balance of weight

Divide your weight between "seat and feet." Part of your weight should be on the bench and part on your left foot. This division of weight helps you feel comfortably balanced and free to play over the entire keyboard without moving up or down on the bench.

Hand Position

The pictures and comments which follow will remind you of what you learned about a good hand position in Books 1 and 2.

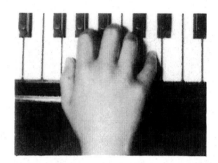

Picture 1 shows the right hand as it looks from above:

–the knuckles of the four fingers are visible

–the thumb is loose and curved slightly toward the 2nd finger

–the fingertips form a curved shape on the keyboard, like this:

Picture 2 shows the right hand as it looks from the thumb's side:

–the arch is high and level, not slopng toward the fifth finger

–the thumb is close to the 2nd finger and curving slightly toward it

Picture 3 shows the right hand as it looks from the 5th finger's side:

–the arch is high and level

–the 5th finger is standing tall with a firm tip

Keyboard Topography

Physical readiness to play also involves careful consideration of keyboard topography—the study of how your hands and fingers adjust to accommodate the configurations of white and black keys in various positions. When a position includes black keys, prepare your hand over the black keys *first,* then allow your hand to settle comfortably onto the white keys. Preparing the black keys first avoids the excess motion or tension caused by "reaching" for the black keys.

Preparing the Keyboard Topography of D Major

Preparing the black key first:

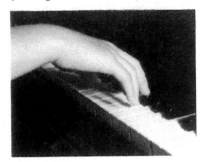

Settling into position:

Comparing the Keyboard Topography of G Major with G♭ Major

Notice the dramatic difference between the keys of G Major and G♭ Major. In G♭, the hand is higher because the black keys are higher and it is farther forward because the black keys are shorter.

Right Hand in G Major
(1 and 5 on whites)

Right Hand in G♭ Major
(1 and 5 on blacks)

Preparing the Topography of an A Major Scale Crossing

In this picture, the right hand is playing a descending A Major scale. The thumb has played and fingers 4-3-2 are prepared as a unit over G#-F#-E.

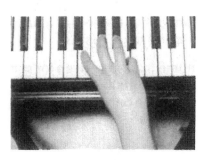

Impulse Practice

Impulse practice means playing a musical gesture with one uninterrupted motion of the arm. The notes within the gesture are carried out by the fingers. Begin with enough energy to carry you through the gesture on a single impulse.

Play-Prepare

Play-prepare is a term we use to describe the most efficient and musical way to move from one position to another. It means that the energy used to play a given gesture also prepares the hand for what comes next. Whenever play-prepare is to be used, an asterisk (*) shows you exactly when to be prepared for the next position.

How to Use This Book

Abbreviations

Throughout this book, RH means right hand, LH means left hand and HT means hands together.

Memorizing

As in Books 1 and 2, the exercises in this book are patterns that are easy to remember. We recommend that you memorize the patterns at once so that instead of reading them, your eyes can focus on your hands and you can concentrate fully on how they *look* and *feel* to make the desired sounds.

Most of the patterns are to be played many times—by repeating them; by playing them in different octaves; by playing them on each consecutive key within an octave; or by transposing them to many different keys.

Dynamics

Signs for loud and soft are given only when the exercise calls for two contrasting dynamic levels simultaneously. Elsewhere, your teacher will assign the dynamic level appropriate for specific patterns in any given lesson.

Tempo

At first, practice the patterns so slowly that you can concentrate on the desired *sound, look* and *feel*. When a pattern is secure at a slow tempo, gradually increase your tempo, but never play a pattern faster than you can play it with complete rhythmic and tonal control.

Metronome marks are given for some of the patterns, but we do *not* recommend that you practice with the metronome. Instead we suggest that you and your teacher use the metronome only to determine what we mean by slow tempo or fast tempo for any given exercise.

Rhythm

A strong rhythmic pulse and flow is essential to all technical practice. Before beginning to practice any pattern, feel the pulse so strongly that it will maintain itself to the end of the exercise.

Daily Practice

In developing any physical skill, practice must be regular. Piano practice is no exception. Daily practice is essential to developing the technic necessary for the music you want to play. As your technic becomes more comfortable, efficient and musical, playing the piano will be more and more rewarding.

Frances Clark, Louise Goss and Sam Holland

Acknowledgements

We gratefully acknowledge our photographic models, Gregory Gordon, Elaine Cheng and Vivian Tso; also the students of the New School for Music Study who tested pilot editions and our teaching staff who taught, criticized and contributed to the present edition. Special thanks to students, staff and colleagues too numerous to name who, for twenty years, have helped in the development of the ideas and materials presented in this book.

Contents

Five-Finger Positions

A. Developing Facility in Sixteenth Notes

1. Contrary Motion

As you play pattern 1:

In measures 1-2, emphasize the tones played by fingers 5, 4, 3, 2.
Play your thumb with a gentle, weightless feeling.
In measures 4-5, emphasize the tones played by fingers 1, 2, 3, 4.
Play your 5th finger with a gentle, weightless feeling.

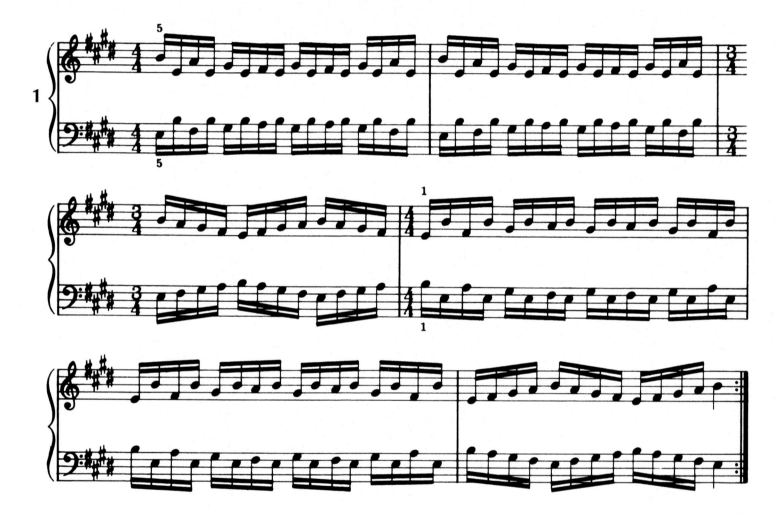

SOUND & FEEL   In measure 4, did you hear and feel the emphasis change from fingers 5, 4, 3, 2 to fingers 1, 2, 3, 4?

Play pattern 1 again, this time in E *minor.*

2. Parallel Motion

Patterns 2a-b use the same notes as pattern 1, but in *parallel* motion.
As you play them:

Emphasize the tones played by fingers 5, 4, 3, 2 or 1, 2, 3, 4.
Play your thumb or 5th finger with a gentle, weightless feeling.

Play patterns 2a-b again, this time in E *minor*.

B. Keyboard Topography—A Review

When a position includes black keys, prepare your hand for the black keys first, so that your hands and fingers fit the topography naturally.

Study the pictures below, comparing D♭ major with D major:

In D♭ major, only one finger is on a *white* key.

In D major, only one finger is on a *black* key.

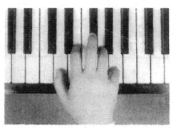

Notice that in D♭ major, with fingers 1 and 5 on black keys, the hand is higher and farther forward than it is in D major.

Before playing pattern 3, compare the look and feel of D♭ major with D major by moving your hand back and forth from one position to the other.

Then play pattern 3:

    RH alone
    LH alone
    HT

Transpose pattern 3 to each of the pairs of keys listed below.

Before playing, compare the look and feel of each pair of keys by moving your hand back and forth from one position to the other.

F MAJOR

In F major, which one finger plays a *black* key?

LH ____ RH ____

F# MAJOR

In F# major, which one finger plays a *white* key?

LH ____ RH ____

E MAJOR

In E major, which two fingers play *black* keys?

LH ____ ____ RH ____ ____

E♭ MAJOR

In E♭ major, which two fingers play *white* keys?

LH ____ ____ RH ____ ____

In the pairs of keys above, both fingers 1 and 5 are on white keys or both are on black keys.

In the keys of B♭ major and B major, finger 1 *or* finger 5 is on a black key, but not both.

B♭ MAJOR

In B♭ major, which two fingers play *black* keys?

LH ____ ____ RH ____ ____

B MAJOR

In B major, which two fingers play *white* keys?

LH ____ ____ RH ____ ____

For further experience in keyboard topography, turn back to patterns 1 and 2a-b, and transpose them to each pair of keys listed above.

C. Changing Keyboard Topography within a Pattern

Before playing patterns 4a-b:

    Practice the moves silently until secure.

    Be sure each move is *direct* and *graceful*.

The asterisk (*) shows exactly when to be prepared for the next position.

Play patterns 4a-b:

    RH alone

    LH alone (2 octaves lower)

    HT (2 octaves apart)

Play slowly until secure (not faster than ♩ = M.M. 60)

Then play at a fast tempo (goal: ♩ = M.M. 104-120)

In pattern 4a, which fingers are on black keys:

measure 1	LH ___ ___	RH ___ ___	
measure 2	LH ___ ___ ___	RH ___ ___ ___	
measure 3	LH ___ ___ ___ ___	RH ___ ___ ___ ___	
measure 4	LH ___ ___ ___ ___	RH ___ ___ ___	

In pattern 4b, which fingers are on black keys:

measure 1	LH ___ ___ ___ ___	RH ___ ___ ___ ___	
measure 2	LH ___ ___ ___ ___	RH ___ ___ ___ ___	
measure 3	LH ___ ___ ___	RH ___ ___ ___	
measure 4	LH ___ ___	RH ___ ___	

D. Major Five-Finger Positions, Moving Chromatically

In pattern 5, beats 1-2 of each measure are in one position,
and beats 3-4 move to the position a half-step higher.

Study the pictures below.

RH 5th finger has played, thumb is prepared for the next position

RH thumb has played, fingers 2, 3, 4, 5 are prepared for the next position

RH starting position

Play pattern 5:

    RH alone (on beat 2, prepare the thumb for the next position;
                  on beat 3, prepare the whole hand for the next position)

    LH alone (on beat 2, prepare finger 5 for the next position;
                  on beat 3, prepare the whole hand for the next position)

    HT (1 octave apart)

Now play pattern 5 again, changing each 5-finger pattern to *minor*.

2 Scales

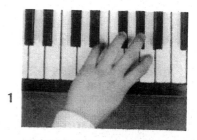

A. E Major Scale

Study these pictures of the LH.

Picture 1 shows how the hand looks when fingers 4-3-2 have crossed over the thumb, or the thumb has passed under fingers 2-3-4.

Picture 2 shows how the hand looks when fingers 3-2 have crossed over the thumb, or the thumb has passed under fingers 2-3.

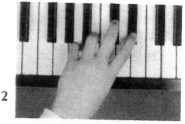

1. LH Preparatory Exercises

Pattern 6 prepares your hand for the topography of the E major scale.

Play each part of the pattern until it feels natural and comfortable—first silently, then with sound.

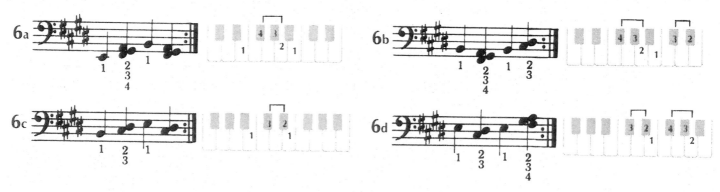

Now play the entire pattern with perfect legato until it feels natural and comfortable.

2. LH Scale

Play the E major scale (pattern 7) up and down 2 octaves at a moderate tempo.

In crossing over, be sure your thumb rolls so that your fingers cross freely over it, preparing the keys as a unit.

In sliding under, be sure your arch is high and that your thumb is loose and travels behind each finger as it plays.

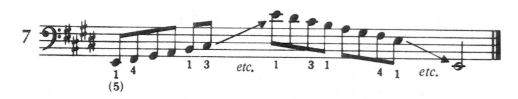

SOUND	Did you play legato, with a full, even tone and steady rhythm?
FEEL	Did your thumb roll loosely so that your fingers crossed freely over it?
LOOK	Did your thumb travel behind each finger as it played?

Study these pictures of the RH.

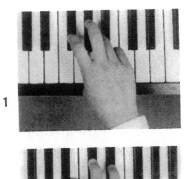

Picture 1 shows how the hand looks when
fingers 3-2 have crossed over the thumb,
or the thumb has passed under fingers 2-3.

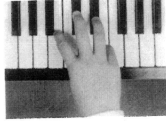

Picture 2 shows how the hand looks when
fingers 4-3-2 have crossed over the thumb,
or the thumb has passed under fingers 2-3-4.

3. RH Preparatory Exercises

Pattern 8 prepares your hand for the topography of the E major scale.

Play each part of the pattern until it feels natural and comfortable—
first silently, then with sound.

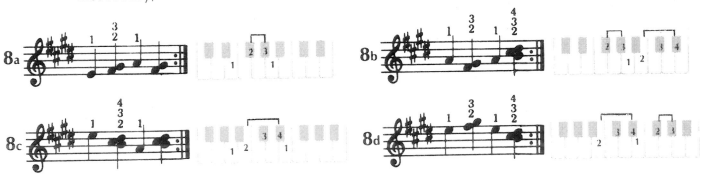

Now play the entire pattern with perfect legato until it feels natural and comfortable.

4. RH Scale

Play the E major scale (pattern 9) up and down 2 octaves at a moderate tempo.
   In sliding under, be sure your arch is high and that your thumb is loose
   and travels behind each finger as it plays.
   In crossing over, be sure your thumb rolls so that your fingers
   cross freely over it, preparing the keys as a unit.

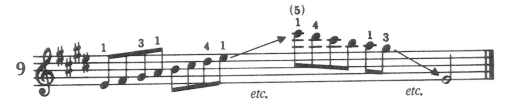

5. HT Scale

Play the entire scale HT up and down 4 octaves at a moderate tempo.

SOUND
FEEL   } Answer the questions at the bottom of page 16.
LOOK

6. Impulse Practice*

Pattern 10 provides practice in fast impulses for each part of the E Major scale.

Practice Steps

1. Play each group of sixteenth notes as rapidly as possible,
   with light, clear articulation, pausing to relax on each ⌢.
   Begin each group of sixteenth notes with enough energy to
   carry you to the next ⌢ on *one* impulse.

2. Play the entire pattern (without pausing on the ⌢), as rapidly
   and clearly as possible.

   RH alone
   LH alone (2 octaves lower)
   HT (2 octaves apart)

7. Building Tempo

Play the entire scale up and down in each of the rhythms started below:
   RH alone
   LH alone (1 octave lower)
   HT (1 octave apart)

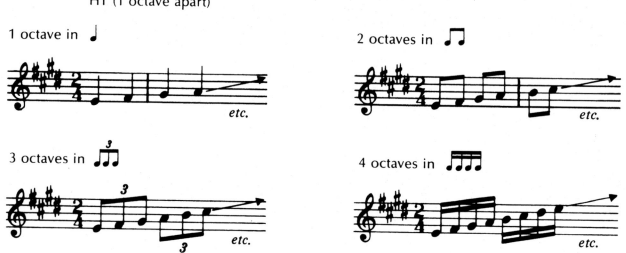

*See Preface, page 6.

B. E♭ Major Scale

Study these pictures of the LH.

Picture 1 shows how the hand looks when fingers 4-3-2 have crossed over the thumb, or the thumb has passed under fingers 2-3-4.

Picture 2 shows how the hand looks when fingers 3-2 have crossed over the thumb, or the thumb has passed under fingers 2-3.

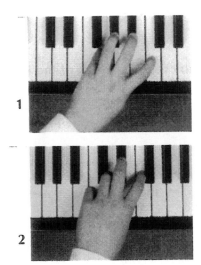

1. LH Preparatory Exercises

Pattern 11 prepares your hand for the topography of the E♭ major scale.

Play each part of the pattern until it feels natural and comfortable—first silently, then with sound.

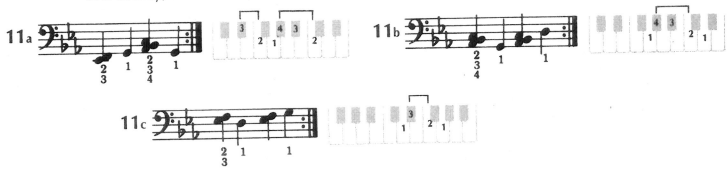

Now play the entire pattern with perfect legato until it feels natural and comfortable.

2. LH Scale

Play the E♭ major scale (pattern 12) up and down 2 octaves at a moderate tempo.

In crossing over, be sure your thumb rolls so that your fingers cross freely over it, preparing the keys as a unit.

In sliding under, be sure your arch is high and that your thumb is loose and travels behind each finger as it plays.

SOUND	Did you play legato, with a full, even tone and steady rhythm?
FEEL	Did your thumb roll loosely so that your fingers crossed freely over it?
LOOK	Did your thumb travel behind each finger as it played?

Study these pictures of the RH.

Picture 1 shows how the hand looks when
fingers 3-2 have crossed over the thumb,
or the thumb has passed under fingers 2-3.

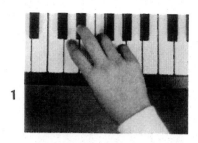
1

Picture 2 shows how the hand looks when
fingers 4-3-2 have crossed over the thumb,
or the thumb has passed under fingers 2-3-4.

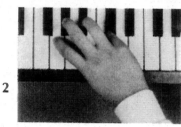
2

3. RH Preparatory Exercises

Pattern 13 prepares your hand for the topography of the E♭ major scale.

Play each part of the pattern until it feels natural and comfortable—
first silently, then with sound.

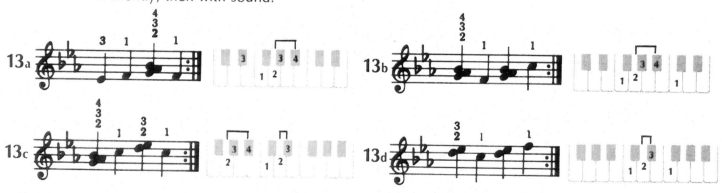

Now play the entire pattern with perfect legato until it feels natural
and comfortable.

4. RH Scale

Play the E♭ major scale (pattern 14) up and down 2 octaves at a
moderate tempo.

In sliding under, be sure your arch is high and that your thumb
is loose and travels behind each finger as it plays.

In crossing over, be sure your thumb rolls so that your fingers
cross freely over it, preparing the keys as a unit.

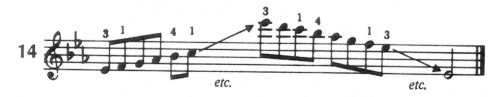

5. HT Scale

Play the entire scale HT up and down 4 octaves at a moderate tempo.

SOUND
FEEL   }   Answer the questions at the bottom of page 19.
LOOK

6. Impulse Practice

Pattern 15 provides practice in fast impulses for each part of the Eᵇ Major scale.

Practice Steps

1. Play each group of sixteenth notes as rapidly as possible, with light, clear articulation, pausing to relax on each ⌒. Begin each group of sixteenth notes with enough energy to carry you to the next ⌒ on *one* impulse.

2. Play the entire pattern (without pausing on the ⌒), as rapidly and clearly as possible.

    RH alone
    LH alone (2 octaves lower)
    HT (2 octaves apart)

7. Building Tempo

Play the entire scale up and down in each of the rhythms started below:

    RH alone
    LH alone (1 octave lower)
    HT (1 octave apart)

1 octave in

etc.

2 octaves in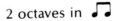

etc.

3 octaves in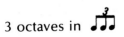

etc.

4 octaves in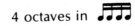

etc.

22

3 Arpeggios

A. Preparation through Melodic Triads and Inversions

To produce a full, rich tone in extended positions:

Allow your wrist to move laterally so that each finger aligns
with the key as it plays.
Never stretch farther or remain stretched longer than necessary.

Study these pictures of the LH:

Finger 5 has played
and 4 is prepared

Finger 4 has played
and 2 is prepared

Finger 2 has played
and 1 is prepared

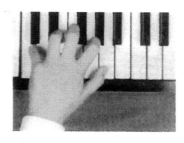 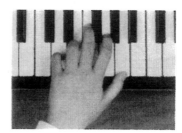 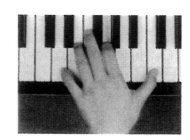

Play pattern 16:
LH alone
RH alone (2 octaves higher)
HT (2 octaves apart)

SOUND   Did each tone sound equally full and rich?
LOOK   Did your wrist move laterally so that each finger aligned
with the key as it played?

Transpose pattern 16 to each of the keys listed below:

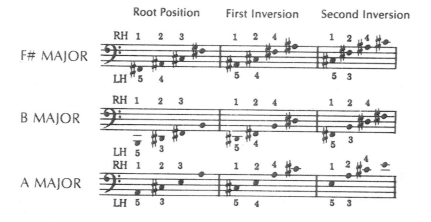

Play patterns 17a-c:
  RH alone
  LH alone (2 octaves lower)
  HT (2 octaves apart)

SOUND   Answer the questions on page 22.
& LOOK

Transpose patterns 17a-c to each of these keys:
  F# MAJOR   B MAJOR   C MAJOR

Play pattern 18:
  LH alone
  RH alone (2 octaves higher)

Play pattern 18 in each of these rhythms:

![rhythm notation]

Transpose pattern 18 and its alternate rhythms to each of these keys:
  F# MAJOR   B MAJOR   D MAJOR

B. G Major Arpeggio

Arpeggios involve skill in crossings very much
like that of scales, but require extended positions
and larger distances for the fingers to travel in
crossing.

1

Study these pictures:

Picture 1 shows how the RH looks when fingers
3-2 have crossed over the thumb or when the
thumb has passed under finger 3.
Note that finger 2 is *not* reaching for B.

Picture 2 shows how the RH looks when finger 3
has played and fingers 2-1 are prepared.

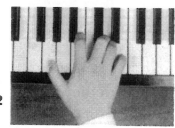

2

1. RH Preparatory Exercises

Patterns 19a-c prepare your RH for the extended crossing in the
G Major arpeggio.

In pattern 19a, be sure your thumb rolls freely so that your
fingers cross directly on the surface of the keys, not in the air.

In pattern 19b, be sure your thumb slides loosely on the surface
of the keys.

Play patterns 19a-b until they feel natural and comfortable—
first silently, then with sound.

Play pattern 19c until it feels natural and comfortable.
Be sure your thumb travels behind each finger as it plays.

2. RH Arpeggio in 4 Octaves

Play the G Major arpeggio up and down 4 octaves in each
of the rhythms started below:

3. LH Preparatory Exercises

Patterns 21a-c prepare your LH for the extended crossing in the
G Major arpeggio.

In pattern 21a, be sure your thumb rolls freely so that your
fingers cross directly on the surface of the keys, not in the air.

In pattern 21b, be sure your thumb slides loosely on the
surface of the keys.

Play patterns 21a-b until they feel natural and comfortable—
first silently, then with sound.

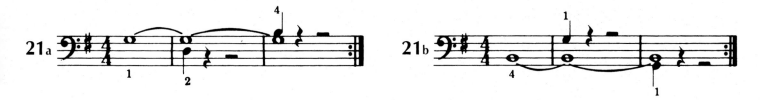

Play pattern 21c until it feels natural and comfortable.

Be sure your thumb travels behind each finger as it plays.

4. LH Arpeggio in 4 Octaves

Play the G Major arpeggio up and down 4 octaves in
each of the rhythms started below:

5. HT Arpeggio in 4 Octaves

Play the G Major arpeggio HT up and down 4 octaves in each of the
rhythms above.

Practice arpeggios in each of the keys listed below:
HT up and down 4 octaves, in each of the rhythms above.

			Fingering
C MAJOR	F MAJOR	E MINOR	RH: 1-2-3-1 LH: 1-4-2-1
A MAJOR	B MAJOR	D MAJOR	RH: 1-2-3-1 LH: 1-3-2-1

Consecutive Double Notes

A. Thirds

1. Legato Thirds in a Five-Finger Position

Play pattern 23 until it flows easily (♩ = M.M. 60):
RH alone
LH alone (1 octave lower)

SOUND   Within each slur were the two voices legato?

Transpose pattern 23 to each of these keys:

F MAJOR   F MINOR   E MAJOR   E MINOR

2. Legato Thirds in Extended Positions

Patterns 24a-d provide experience in playing legato thirds between fingers $\frac{3}{1}$ and $\frac{2}{1}$.
Play each pattern, beginning on every white key within one octave.

RH alone descending

RH alone ascending

LH alone ascending

LH alone descending

SOUND   Were the two voices legato throughout, especially
between fingers $\frac{3}{1}$ and $\frac{2}{1}$?

3. Staccato Thirds in Extended Positions

Play patterns 25a-f up and down in 3 different octaves.

For RH alone

For LH alone

Transpose patterns 25a-f to the keys of F MAJOR and C MAJOR.

B. Sixths

1. Legato Sixths

In pattern 26a, substituting fingers 5-4 or 4-5 makes it possible to play the *upper* voice legato.

> After the thumb plays, finger 4 replaces finger 5 *ascending* and finger 5 replaces finger 4 *descending*.

For RH alone—play on every white key up and down from C to C.

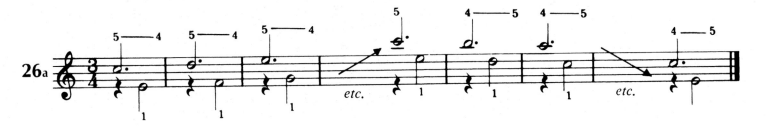

Pattern 26b provides experience in playing *both* voices legato.
To play the *lower* voice as legato as possible, slide your thumb.

In pattern 27b, substituting fingers 5-4 or 4-5 makes it possible to play the *lower* voice legato.

> After the thumb plays, finger 4 replaces finger 5 *descending* and finger 5 replaces finger 4 *ascending*.

For LH alone—play on every white key down and up from C to C.

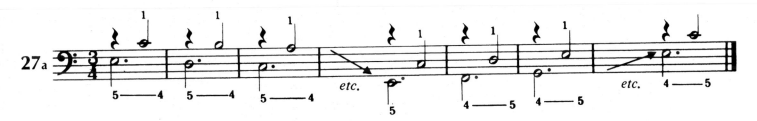

Pattern 27b provides experience in playing *both* voices legato.
To play the *upper* voice as legato as possible, slide your thumb.

2. Rapid Consecutive Sixths

To play consecutive 6ths rapidly, you need a firm arch, strong tips and a loose wrist.

A firm arch and strong tips result in clear, precise tones.
A loose wrist allows your hand to rebound into the next 6th.

The small notes should be played very rapidly and lightly, just *before* the beat. Both the double and triple upbeats should take the same amount of time.

Play patterns 28a-b:
RH alone
LH alone (2 octaves lower)

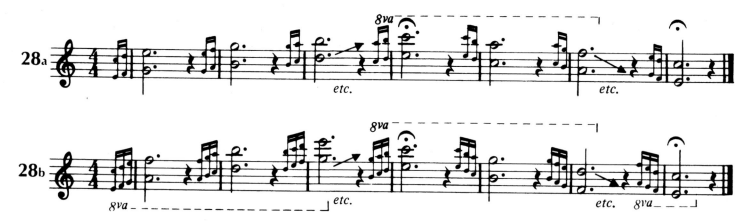

C. Octaves

1. Octave Reaches

To reach an octave comfortably, keep your hand as loose and supple as possible. In pattern 29:

Slide your thumb or 5th finger to the new position without leaving the surface of the key.
Once the pattern is started, be sure you always hear two tones—octave, 7th, octave, 7th, etc.

Play pattern 29 up and down on every white key from C to C:
RH alone
LH alone (2 octaves lower)

2. Broken Octaves

Play pattern 30 legato, on every key of the chromatic scale from C to C:
RH alone
LH alone (2 octaves lower)

In pattern 31, keep your hand in motion, never "fixing" in an octave reach—it is always in the process of extending or contracting so that finger 1 replaces 5 or 5 replaces 1.

Play pattern 31 on every key of the chromatic scale from C to C:

    RH alone
    LH alone (2 octaves lower)

3. Rapid Consecutive and Repeated Octaves

In patterns 32a-b, the small notes should be played very rapidly and lightly, just *before* the beat. Both the single and double upbeats should take the same amount of time.

Play patterns 32a-b up and down on every white key from C to C:

    RH alone
    LH alone (2 octaves lower)
    HT (2 octaves apart)

Facility: Impulse Practice in Special Patterns

A. Developing Facility within a Five-Finger Position

1. Facility Practice for RH

Play pattern 33 *slowly* (not faster than ♩ = M.M. 60) until secure.

To be able to play pattern 33 at a fast tempo, practice fingers 5, 4, 3 as a *fast impulse* (not slower than ♩ = M.M. 104) in each of the steps outlined below.

a) *Fingers 54345*

1 beat + 1 note: 2 beats + 1 note:

3 beats + 1 note:

Follow the same steps for patterns b), c) and d), playing each of them as *fast impulses* of 1, 2 and 3 beats.

b) *Fingers 34543*   c) *Fingers 45434*   d) *Fingers 43454*

Now play pattern 33 at a *fast tempo* (goal: ♩ = M.M. 104).

For further practice in developing facility with fingers 5, 4, 3, play pattern 33 in each of these keys:

F MAJOR   F MINOR   E♭ MAJOR   E♭ MINOR

2. *Facility Practice for LH*

Play pattern 34 *slowly* (not faster than ♩ = M.M. 60) until secure.

To be able to play pattern 34 at a fast tempo, practice fingers 5, 4, 3 as a *fast impulse* (not slower than ♩ = M.M. 104) in each of the steps outlined below.

a) *Fingers 54345*

1 beat + 1 note   2 beats + 1 note

3 beats + 1 note

Follow the same steps for patterns b), c), d), playing each of them as *fast impulses* of 1, 2 and 3 beats.

b) *Fingers 34543*   c) *Fingers 45434*   d) *Fingers 43454*

Now play pattern 34 at a *fast tempo* (goal: ♩ = M.M. 104).

For further practice in developing facility with fingers 5, 4, 3, play pattern 34 in each of these keys:

E MAJOR   E MINOR   F# MAJOR   F# MINOR

B. Developing Facility in Extended Passages

Play pattern 35 *slowly* (♩ = M.M. 60) on every white key from C to C:

    RH alone
    LH alone (1 octave lower)
    HT (1 octave apart)

To be able to play pattern 35 at a fast tempo, practice it in *fast impulses* (not slower than ♩ = M.M 104):

    1 measure + 1 note
    2 measures + 1 note

Then play the entire pattern at a *fast tempo* (goal: ♩ = M.M. 104).

Use the same steps for practicing pattern 36.

For further practice, play patterns 35-36 in each of these rhythms:

C. Facility In Extending to the Octave

In patterns 37a-39b:

> Keep a "light" hand and articulate precisely with each finger.
> Rotate freely as if "shaking out" the notes.
> Emphasize the thumb with a little extra weight.

For RH alone—play slowly *(not faster than* ♩ *= M.M. 60) until secure.*

To be able to play pattern 37a at a fast tempo, practice it in *fast impulses* (not slower than ♩ = M.M. 104):

each measure + 1 note:

each 2 measures + 1 note:

Now play the entire pattern at a *fast tempo* (goal: ♩ = M.M. 104).

For LH alone—play slowly *(not faster than* ♩ *= M.M. 60) until secure.*

To be able to play pattern 37b at a fast tempo, practice it in *fast impulses* (not slower than ♩ = M.M. 104):

each measure + 1 note:

each 2 measures + 1 note:

Now play the entire pattern at a *fast tempo* (goal: ♩ = M.M. 104).

SOUND   Did you emphasize the thumb slightly?
FEEL   Did you keep a "light" hand?
   Did you rotate freely as if "shaking out" the notes?

Transpose patterns 37a-b to each of these keys:

     E MAJOR   E♭ MAJOR   B MAJOR   B♭ MAJOR

Play each of the following patterns *slowly* (♩ = M.M. 60) until secure.

When each pattern is secure at a slow tempo, follow the steps for fast impulse practice outlined on page 33.

For RH alone

For LH alone

Play pattern 39a:
  RH alone
  LH alone (2 octaves lower)

Play pattern 39b:
  LH alone
  RH alone (2 octaves higher)

Transpose patterns 38a-39b to each of these keys:

E MAJOR   E♭ MAJOR   B MAJOR   B♭ MAJOR

 # Miscellaneous

A. Developing Finger Independence

The goal of patterns 40a-42b is to develop the ability to play any finger without causing motion or tension in any other finger.

In each pattern:

  Play the tied note and hold it with just enough pressure to keep the key depressed throughout the pattern.

  Be sure there is motion only in the finger that is playing, and not in any other finger.

1. Sustaining Finger 2

For RH alone

40a

For LH alone

40b

2. Sustaining Finger 4

For RH alone

41a

For LH alone

41b

3. Sustaining Finger 3

For RH alone

42a

For LH alone

42b

LOOK   Was there motion only in the finger that was playing?

FEEL   Did you hold the tied note very lightly, with just enough pressure to keep the key depressed?

For further experience in finger independence, transpose patterns 40a-42b to each of these keys:

D MAJOR   D♭ MAJOR   B MAJOR   B♭ MAJOR

B. Two Simultaneous Voices in One Hand

In patterns 43a-44b, both voices are legato, but one voice is *forte* while the other is *piano*.

Play each pattern, listening for legato and for contrast in dynamic levels.

1. Outside Voice Forte, Inside Voice Piano

For RH alone

For LH alone

2. Inside Voice Forte, Outside Voice Piano

For RH alone

For LH alone

SOUND   In each pattern, did both voices sound legato?
Did you hear the contrast in dynamic level between voices?

Now play patterns 43a-44b, highlighting the difference between voices by using each of the articulations shown below.

C. Rapid Repeated Notes

Changing fingers will help you play repeated notes rapidly and clearly.

Play patterns 45a-46b at a fast tempo (goal: ♩ = M.M. 112), keeping your hand as loose as possible.

1. Fingers 321 on Repeated Notes

For RH alone

For LH alone

2. Fingers 4321 on Repeated Notes

For RH alone

For LH alone

SOUND   Were the repeated notes rapid and clear?

FEEL   Did your hand feel loose as you played the repeated notes?

D. Embellishments: Turns and Mordents

Turns and mordents are embellishments—notes that are not essential
to the melody, but are used to decorate it. They are usually played very
rapidly and with clear articulation.

1. Turns

Pattern 47 is designed to help you gain facility in playing turns.

For RH alone

Now play pattern 47 again in this rhythm:

Then transpose pattern 47 to the keys of F MAJOR and C MAJOR.

2. Mordents

Pattern 48 is designed to help you gain facility in playing mordents.
Mordents begin *on* the beat, not before.
Be sure to emphasize the *first* note of the mordent, not the last.

For RH alone

Now play pattern 48 using each of these combinations of fingers:
4343, 5454, 2121

Also play it on:
two black keys (D#-C#)
a white key and a black key (G-F#)
a black key and a white key (B♭-A)

E. Chords

1. Triads and Inversions: Blocked

Play patterns 49-50:
> RH alone
> LH alone (1 octave lower)
> HT (1 octave apart)

Your teacher will assign the fingering appropriate for your hand.

Transpose patterns 49-50 to each of these keys:
> C MAJOR   F# MAJOR   E♭ MAJOR

2. Diminished 7th Chords

Play pattern 51:
> RH alone
> LH alone (2 octaves lower)
> HT (2 octaves apart)

All chords are fingered 1-2-3-5 in both hands.
Be sure all the notes of each chord sound and release exactly together.
The * shows on what beat to be prepared for the next position.

3. Diminished 7th Chords in Octave Moves

Play each of the chords in pattern 51 up and down 3 octaves as shown below:
> RH alone
> LH alone (1 octave lower)
> HT (1 octave apart)

F. Canon

As you learned in Books 1 and 2, a "canon" is a musical form in which the melody is started in one voice, then imitated in another voice.

In each phrase, be sure the LH imitates the RH exactly, not only in notes and rhythm, but also in staccato, slurs, dynamics and accents.

John LaMontaine

Play pattern 52 again, this time in A *minor*.
Then transpose it to the keys of C major and C minor.

From Copycats *by John LaMontaine*
Reprinted by permission of Fredonia Press